# BEAVER

## By Lee Jacobs

BLACKBIRCH®
PRESS

THOMSON
————✦————
GALE

San Diego • Detroit • New York • San Francisco • Cleveland • New Haven, Conn. • Waterville, Maine • London • Munich

THOMSON
GALE

*For more information, contact*
The Gale Group, Inc.
27500 Drake Rd.
Farmington Hills, MI 48331-3535
Or you can visit our Internet site at http://www.gale.com

Photo Credits: cover, pages 3, 7, 14, 15 © Thomas Kitchin & Victoria Hurst; pages 4, 16-17, 22 © CORBIS; pages 5, 6, 8-9, 10-11, 13, 18-19, 20-21 © Tom and Pat Leeson Nature Wildlife Photography; page 23 © Reuel R. Sutton, California Academy of Sciences

**LIBRARY OF CONGRESS CATALOGING-IN-PUBLICATION DATA**

Jacobs, Lee.
 Beaver / by Lee Jacobs.
  p. cm. — (Wild America series)
 Summary: Examines the beaver's environment, physical characteristics, social life, hunting and mating behavior, and encounters with humans.
 Includes bibliographical references and index.
 ISBN 1-56711-566-7 (hardback : alk. paper)
 1. Beavers—Juvenile literature. [1. Beavers.] I. Title.
 QL737.R632 J33 2003
 599.37—dc21                                2002011725

Printed in China
10 9 8 7 6 5 4 3 2 1

# Contents

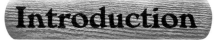

# Introduction

Beavers are rodents that are part of the order Rodentia and the family Castoridae. There are only two species of beaver. One lives in Europe and Asia. The other makes its home throughout Canada and the United States. It is called either the American or Canadian beaver. The scientific name of the North American species is Castor canadensis.

Beavers are rodents. They live throughout the United States and Canada, as well as in Europe and Asia.

A few of the beaver's rodent relatives are squirrels, gophers, and pocket mice. Almost half of all species of mammals are rodents. Rodents have two pairs of large, sharp front teeth called incisors. These teeth, which look a bit like chisels, are designed to gnaw. Rodents also have smaller cheek teeth that they use to chew. Like all rodents, beavers gnaw and chew a lot.

A beaver uses its incisors to gnaw on a branch.

The beaver is the biggest rodent in North America. Beavers are about 24 to 26 inches (61 to 66 cm) long, and their tails add another 12 to 16 inches (30 to 41 cm). An adult of average size usually weighs between 35 and 60 pounds (16 to 27 kg). On all fours, beavers stand only about 12 inches (30 cm) tall.

Beavers spend most of their lives in water. Their bodies are well suited for this. Their large, webbed back feet help them swim. They have black, wide, flat tails that they use in much the same way that people use a rudder to steer a boat. Beavers' bodies are nearly waterproof! Their dark brown or reddish brown fur is soft and thick. It is covered with a layer of coarse guard hairs that shed water.

The average beaver is 24 to 26 inches (61 to 66 cm) long.

Beavers also coat themselves with waterproof oil that their bodies produce. A beaver can close its nostrils, ear openings, and throat to keep out water. Beavers are able to see underwater with the help of an extra pair of clear eyelids that cover their eyes like swimming goggles. Even a beaver's lungs are made for water life. They can hold enough air to allow the beaver to stay underwater for up to 15 minutes! Most often, though, beavers hold their breath for only about 2 minutes at a time.

Beavers build amazing homes out of wood. Their incisor teeth are the sharp tools they use to do this. A rodent's incisors grow throughout its life. A coating of enamel keeps the front of the incisors hard, but the backs of the teeth are soft. They wear down quickly to create a razor-sharp edge.

Like all rodents, beavers have an open space between their top incisors and their back teeth. If it gathers its lips into this gap, a beaver can close its mouth and leave only the incisors outside. This lets the beaver gnaw through a tree and not have its mouth fill up with wood chips. It also lets the beaver whittle wood in the water but not swallow any liquid.

A beaver is able to keep water out of its nostrils, ears, and throat while swimming.

# The Beaver's Environment

Beavers build their homes, called lodges, in ponds that they create right in the middle of rivers and streams. They make these ponds by building dams that trap water. Most of this work is done in the dark, since beavers are nocturnal animals that sleep during the day and are active at night.

Beavers make ponds in water sources that are in or close to woods. To build a dam, a beaver gnaws down trees and drags a huge amount of wood to the water. Once the wood is near the shore, the beaver moves it into the water. The wood floats, and the beaver guides it to the dam site. Beavers also dig canals about 3 feet (1 m) wide that lead to trees farther from shore. This way, they do not have to carry heavy loads on land. (The canals also help beavers, which are clumsy on land, escape danger quickly.)

A beaver often stands up on its hind feet and uses its wide tail to balance while it gnaws through a tree trunk. (The beaver will also carry small loads in its front paws while it walks upright on its hind legs.) Within a few minutes, a beaver can chew through a tree that is 5 inches (13 cm) thick. Larger, thicker trees take longer to chew. Sometimes, members of a beaver family take turns as they work on a stubborn tree.

Beavers drag huge amounts of wood to the places where they make dams.

Before they pile wood in the water, beavers push large stones and mud together to make a foundation for the dam. Large logs are then laid to build the basic structure of the dam. Smaller branches make up the rest. Twigs, stones, and mud are shoved into any openings to strengthen the dam. To make their dams as watertight as possible, beavers scoop up mud from the riverbed and smear it on the sides of the dam.

Dams are built 5 to 10 feet (2 to 3 m) high and very wide. Some may even stretch as far as 300 feet (91 m) across a river. In addition to the main dam, beavers usually build two others—one upstream and one downstream. Beavers are constantly busy as they repair leaks and work to keep their dams strong. Once the dam is finished and the pond is in place, the lodge is built.

Although most lodges are built in the middle of a beaver pond, some lodges can be found onshore next to a river or lake. From above the water, a lodge looks like a simple mound or dome-shaped pile of branches. Lodges are not simple structures, though. They are carefully designed to be strong, safe, warm, and dry.

Beavers begin to construct their lodge at the river bottom. They pile up stones, mud, and wood until the lodge has a base that is 10 to 15 feet (3 to 5 m) wide. As they build up toward the surface of the water, the beavers make two or more underwater tunnel entrances to the lodge. At the top of one of them, a small area is built a bit lower than the main room. There, a beaver will be able to drip-dry before it enters.

The main room, or den, is built above the water level of the pond. This keeps the den completely dry inside. This room is often about 3 feet (1 m) high and 8 feet (2 m) wide. Soft wood chippings or shredded leafy materials cover the floor. The rounded roof above the den can stretch more than 15 feet (5 m) across. One or more holes in the roof let in fresh air.

Walls up to 3 feet (1 m) thick make the lodge very secure. Beavers plaster cement-like material made from rocks and mud all over the outside of the lodge. This material freezes in the winter and makes the den even safer from attacks by predators (animals that hunt other animals for food). The frozen mud also provides extra protection against the cold.

In the cozy main room, beavers sleep, care for their babies, and stay safely protected from predators. Wolves, coyotes, foxes, mountain lions, and bears threaten beavers on land. In the water, however, the fast-swimming beaver can easily escape most enemies and slip off to its lodge.

The main room of a beaver's lodge is built above water level. Beavers are well protected in this area of their homes.

# Social Life

Beavers live in family groups, called colonies, of about 5 to 15 animals. A colony usually includes an adult male, an adult female, and their offspring from the past two years. Beavers are very social animals. The members of a colony care for each other, groom each other, and work together to build their dams and lodge.

A beaver colony's territory, or home range, reaches about half a mile (0.8 km) up and down the river from the lodge and about 650 feet (198 m) onto the shore. Beavers are territorial. One colony's home range is not open to other beavers. Beavers send a signal to tell others to stay out of their territory. They gather several small piles of mud and scent-mark them with oil made by special glands. Several beavers from the colony add their scents to the mounds. The smell is unmistakable to newcomers. It acts as a "Keep Out" sign!

Beavers communicate with sound as well as scent. They slap their tails hard on the water to make a loud smacking noise. This noise warns other beavers of danger. Beavers may also have other ways to communicate. Many campers and hikers report that they have heard sounds of beaver "talk" that drifts from lodges.

**Opposite page:** Beavers are safest in the water.
**Inset:** Beavers work together in groups to build dams.

## Gatherers

Although beavers have excellent senses of smell and hearing, they cannot see well in the dark. Despite their poor night vision, beavers gather most of their food at night. They are herbivorous, which means they mainly eat plant materials. A beaver's diet is mostly made up of grasses, leaves, stems, tree sap, and bark. Their favorite trees are willow and aspen. In the warmer months, they prefer fresh leaves, grasses, and other green plants. One of a beaver's favorite foods is the water lily.

A beaver carries fresh leaves to its lodge.

During the winter, beavers rely heavily on tree bark for food. To eat it, a beaver holds a branch and turns it while its sharp front teeth strip the nutritious bark from the wood—in much the same way that a person eats corn on the cob. Because beavers cannot climb as their squirrel relatives do, they sometimes fell (knock down) trees to get to the leafy food at the top. Beavers are always careful to stay out of the way when a tree crashes to the ground.

Beavers do not hibernate (sleep through the winter). Once their pond freezes, it is hard for them to reach food sources on land. To solve this problem, beavers store food for the winter. Branches are dragged near the lodge and anchored underwater for later use. The cold winter water helps keep the food fresh.

In winter, beavers eat a lot of tree bark.

# The Mating Game

Both male and female beavers can reproduce by the time they are 2 years of age. Mating season for beavers usually begins in January or February. Female beavers are pregnant for 107 to 110 days. They give birth once a year, generally in late spring or early summer. A female usually has 2 to 8 babies in a litter.

Once a male and female beaver mate, they stay together as partners for life. The male helps care for new babies, as do the young beavers born in the previous year's litter. It is the whole colony's job to help raise the young.

Beavers who mate remain together as partners for life.

# Beaver Babies

A mother beaver gives birth to her babies inside the family's lodge. Baby beavers are called kits. Kits are born with their eyes open, and they have teeth and fur.  They weigh about 1 pound (0.5 kg). The mother nurses her young for 6 weeks.

Kits can swim very well within the first week of their lives, but they do not leave the safety of the lodge for 4 weeks. That is because they are not yet able to dive, which they must do to exit the lodge through its underwater tunnels. If a beaver baby falls into a watery tunnel, an adult will rescue it and dry it off. During the kits' first month of life, the other beavers bring them leaves and bark to eat in the lodge. Every few days, the parents and older beavers clean out the wood chips or grasses used for bedding and replace them with fresh material.

Baby beavers, called kits, nurse for 6 weeks.

After about a month, a beaver colony goes on its first family outing. Kits who get tired while they swim can climb on an adult's back and hitch a ride. The babies learn many skills as they watch the older beavers. Often, this first trip is when the kits learn to dive, as well as how to feed on nearby leaves and bark. When they grow a bit older, they also help the adults store food for the winter.

Kits stay with their parents for up to 2 years, and help raise the next litter of babies. Then they go off on their own to find a new territory, mate, and start their own colony. This leaves room in their parents' colony for the litter of kits that will arrive the next year. In the wild, a beaver can live for 15 to 20 years.

A beaver colony goes on its first outing as a family when new kits are a month old. Kits learn what to eat and how to swim by watching the adult beavers.

Since the 1600s, humans have hunted and trapped beavers for their fur. In fact, trade in beaver fur was so profitable that it played a big role in the early exploration and settlement of the American West. Beaver lodges, which keep the animals safe from wild predators, were easy targets for human hunters. By 1800, so many beavers were killed that the whole species was nearly wiped out. In the early 1900s, people who were concerned about beavers and other endangered animals helped pass laws to protect them.

Humans have hunted and trapped beavers for their fur since the 1600s.

Today, some people view beavers as pests. Beavers have been known to build dams in farmers' irrigation ditches, which floods farmland. In most cases, though, beavers actually improve the natural environment. Beaver dams help control flooding by slowing down the runoff from heavy rains. They also help slow soil erosion by trapping sediment that would otherwise reach larger rivers. Beaver ponds also provide rich habitats for other animals, such as fish, turtles, frogs, insects, muskrats, otters, water birds, and even moose.

People may view beavers as pests, but beaver dams help to control flooding and soil erosion.

# Glossary

**colony** a family group of beavers

**herbivorous** eating mainly plant materials

**hibernate** to sleep through the winter

**kit** a baby beaver

**lodge** the home beavers build

**nocturnal** asleep during the day and active at night

**predator** an animal that hunts other animals for food

# For Further Reading

## Books

Crewe, Sabrina. *The Beaver.* Austin, TX: Raintree/Steck-Vaughn, 1999.

Hodge, Deborah. *Beavers.* Tonawanda, NY: Kids Can Press, 1998.

Martin-James, Kathleen. *Building Beavers.* Minneapolis, MN: Lerner, 1999.

Rounds, Glen. *Beaver.* New York: Holiday House, 1999.

Sullivan, Jody. *Beavers: Big-Toothed Builders.* Mankato, MN: Bridgestone Books, 2002.

# Index